One, Two, Three, Four, Five, Six, Seven!

The Story of Elisha and Naaman

We are grateful to the following team of authors for their contributions to *God Loves Me*, a Bible story program for young children. This Bible story, one of a series of fifty-two, was written by Patricia L. Nederveld, managing editor for CRC Publications. Suggestions for using this book were developed by Jesslyn DeBoer, a freelance author from Grand Rapids, Michigan. Yvonne Van Ee, an early childhood educator, served as project consultant and wrote *God Loves Me*, the program guide that accompanies this series of Bible storybooks.

Nederveld has served as a consultant to Title I early childhood programs in Colorado. She has extensive experience as a writer, teacher, and consultant for federally funded preschool, kindergarten, and early childhood programs in Colorado, Texas, Michigan, Florida, Missouri, and Washington, using the *High/Scope* Education Research Foundation curriculum. In addition to writing the *Bible Footprints* church curriculum for four- and five-year-olds, Nederveld edited the revised *Threes* curriculum and the first edition of preschool through second grade materials for the *LiFE* curriculum, all published by CRC Publications.

DeBoer has served as a church preschool leader and as coauthor of the preschool-kindergarten materials for the *LiFE* curriculum published by CRC Publications. She has also written K-6 science and health curriculum for Christian Schools International, Grand Rapids, Michigan, and inspirational gift books for Zondervan Publishing House.

Van Ee is a professor and early childhood program advisor in the Education Department at Calvin College, Grand Rapids, Michigan. She has served as curriculum author and consultant for Christian Schools International and wrote the original *Story Hour* organization manual and curriculum materials for fours and fives.

Photos on page 5 and 20: SuperStock.

"God Loves Me" is a registered trademark of CRC Publications.

Library of Congress Cataloging-in-Publication Data

Nederveld, Patricia L., 1944-
    One, two , three, four, five, six, seven!: the story of Elisha and Naaman/ Patricia L. Nederveld.
       p. cm. — (God loves me; bk. 21)
    Summary: A simple retelling of the story of how Naaman was cured of leprosy after reluctantly following the advice of Elisha. Includes follow-up activities.
    ISBN 1-56212-290-8
    1. Elisha (Biblical prophet)—Juvenile literature. 2. Naaman, the Syrian—Juvenile literature. 3. Bible stories, English—O.T. Kings, 2nd. 4. Bible games and puzzles. [1. Elisha (Biblical prophet). 2. Naaman, the Syrian. 3. Bible stories—O.T.] I. Title. II. Series: Nederveld, Patricia L., 1944-
God loves me; bk. 21.
BS580.E5N45 1998
222'.5409505—dc21
                                        97-32472
                                            CIP
                                            AC

10 9 8 7 6 5 4 3 2 1

One, Two, Three, Four, Five, Six, Seven!

The Story of Elisha and Naaman

PATRICIA L. NEDERVELD

ILLUSTRATIONS BY LISA WORKMAN

CRC Publications
Grand Rapids, Michigan

This is a story
from God's
book, the Bible.

It's for *say name(s) of your child(ren).*
It's for me too!

2 Kings 5:1-16

Naaman's
skin was
full of sores
that caused him
so much pain.
And not a doctor
in the land
could make him
well again.

But Naaman's little servant said,
"I know what God can do—
now hurry to Elisha.
And God will help you too."

Elisha sent a message
to the sick and hurting man.
"Dip in the river seven times—
this is God's healing plan."

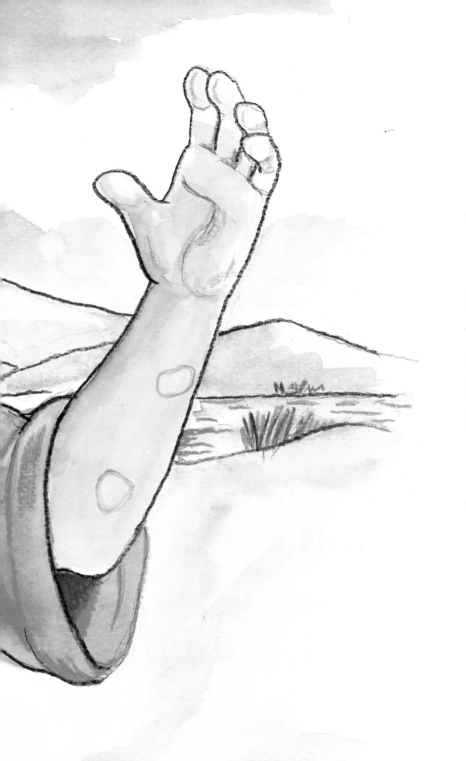

"**N**o way!
Not me!"
said
Naaman
with a loud and
angry cry.
But Naaman's
servants begged
him,
"At least give it
a try!"

He walked down to the river and waded in a bit, then slowly, slowly, slowly down in the water dipped . . .

ONE
  TWO
    THREE
      FOUR
        FIVE
          SIX
            SEVEN...
SEVEN TIMES!

Just then a great thing happened—
it wasn't hard to tell!
And Naaman knew that God was there—
for God had made him well.

Then to Elisha Naaman said, "How wonderful I feel! My skin is fresh and smooth again! I know your God is real!"

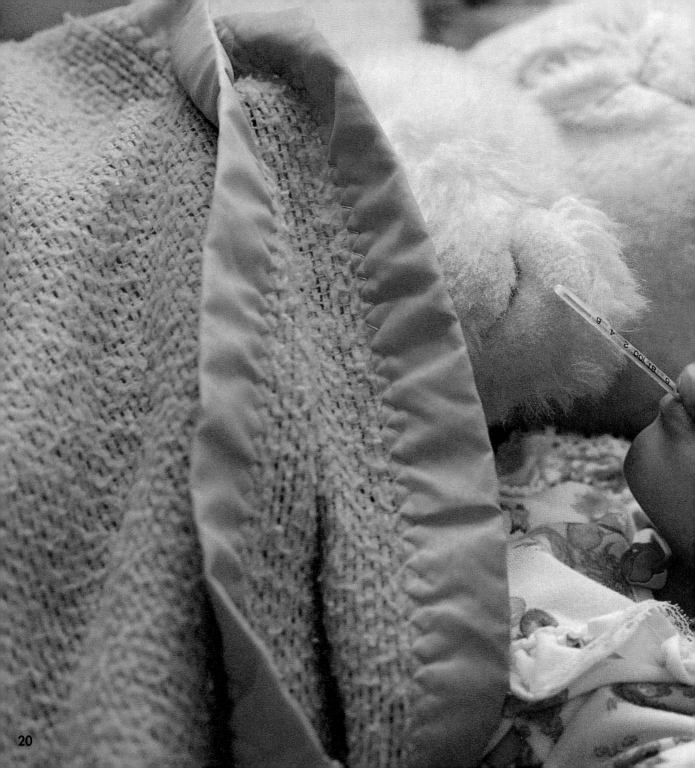

I wonder if you know that our great God can make you well when you're feeling sick . . .

Dear God, thank you for making Naaman well again. We're glad you care for us when we are sick too. Amen.

Suggestions for Follow-up

Opening

Greet your little ones today with words that describe their healthy bodies. As you gather them around you, ask the children if they have ever been hurt or sick. As they recount their stories, tell them how glad you are that God made them well. Assure them that God cares for children, mommies, daddies, grandpas and grandmas—everyone!

Learning Through Play

Learning through play is the best way! The following activity suggestions are meant to help you provide props and experiences that will invite the children to play their way into the Scripture story and its simple truth. Try to provide plenty of time for the children to choose their own activities and to play individually. Use group activities sparingly—little ones learn most comfortably with a minimum of structure.

1. Supply sheets of construction paper and several boxes of Band-Aids of various sizes and shapes. Younger children will probably need help to remove the outer wrappers, but children will enjoy peeling back the tabs and sticking the Band-Aids to the paper—and themselves! You might want to write God Cares for Me on larger Band-Aids and stick one to each child's hand.

2. To encourage dramatic play, provide baby dolls, stuffed animals, and doctor kits. Fill small lunch boxes or old purses with Band-Aids, cotton swabs, tongue depressors or craft sticks, strips of cloth for bandages and casts, and plastic straws for thermometers. To make a simple stethoscope, tape or glue a metal lid from a frozen juice can or a canning lid to one end of a strip of narrow Velcro about 12" (30 cm) long. Separate the two parts of the Velcro to fit around the neck; lap loosely in back so that the strip will come untied easily to prevent choking. (We recommend that you do not include medicine bottles or candy pills in the kits. Young children often do not separate play medicine from the real thing.) Lay out old white shirts or T-shirts for lab coats. Mark off a hospital, clinic, or doctor's office with chairs or building blocks. As you help your young medics wrap hurt limbs and take temperatures, remind the children of God's good care. Model Christlike concern for the sick.

3. Fill a water table with a shallow amount of water, or use a plastic baby bathtub or dishpans. You may want to cover the table with plastic and keep a supply of paper towels handy for wiping up spills. Set out rubber dolls, washcloths, and a fragrant baby shampoo or liquid soap. Children will enjoy scrubbing, sudsing, and splashing the babies. Talk about how clean and healthy the babies look. Ask them if they think Naaman looked clean and healthy after he dipped in the river. Count with the children to seven as they dip their dolls in the water seven times. Remind them that God healed Naaman's sores—the water

helped Naaman feel clean, but God made him well.

4. Invite children to do some exercising as you reenact the part of the story told on pages 14 and 15. Designate a spot in your room or outdoors as the river. Start walking toward the river, and invite the children to join hands and follow along. When you reach the area, pretend to wade in a bit and then slowly, slowly dip in the water seven times. Count slowly to seven as you bend from the waist, touch your toes, or do push-ups. (Remember, your little ones develop coordination at their own pace. You may smile about their form, but you'll marvel at their flexible bones and muscles.) Talk about what hard work dipping was for Naaman when he was sick. Give thanks for your little ones' healthy bodies.

5. Make stick puppets to help your little ones retell the story. Copy the faces of the sick/angry Naaman and the well/happy Naaman (see Pattern H, Patterns Section, *God Loves Me* program guide). Let children scribble color the faces with crayons or sidewalk chalk. Help them glue the angry face to one side of a tongue depressor and then the happy face to the other side of the depressor. Ask your little ones to show and tell how Naaman felt before he dipped in the river. Count to seven. Then ask them to show and tell how Naaman felt after he dipped in the river. Praise God—with your own happy faces—for caring for each child.

Closing

Use your closing time to pray for people who are sick, remembering by name any children who are absent and others the children may have mentioned. Thank God for caring for us when we are sick. You may want to sing some of these stanzas of "God Is So Good" (Songs Section, *God Loves Me* program guide) as children follow your actions:

> *God is so good . . .* (point up)
> *He cares for me . . .* (point to self)
> *Thank you, dear God . . .* (fold hands; sing prayer)
> *We praise you now . . .* (wave crepe paper streamers)
> —Words: Stanzas 1 and 2, traditional

At Home

God cares for your little one! When your child is ill or hurt, your own loving words and actions can convey this message to your child. Young children enjoy playing doctor and nurse with their dolls or stuffed animals. Play along with your child to model Jesus' compassion for the sick. Think of people your child knows who are sick, and pray for them by name at mealtime and bedtime. Encourage your little one to make a card to bring or send to someone who is sick. When your child walks, runs, jumps, climbs—and constantly wiggles—praise God together for a wonderful, healthy body.

Old Testament Stories

Blue and Green and Purple Too! *The Story of God's Colorful World*

It's a Noisy Place! *The Story of the First Creatures*

Adam and Eve *The Story of the First Man and Woman*

Take Good Care of My World! *The Story of Adam and Eve in the Garden*

A Very Sad Day *The Story of Adam and Eve's Disobedience*

A Rainy, Rainy Day *The Story of Noah*

Count the Stars! *The Story of God's Promise to Abraham and Sarah*

A Girl Named Rebekah *The Story of God's Answer to Abraham*

Two Coats for Joseph *The Story of Young Joseph*

Plenty to Eat *The Story of Joseph and His Brothers*

Safe in a Basket *The Story of Baby Moses*

I'll Do It! *The Story of Moses and the Burning Bush*

Safe at Last! *The Story of Moses and the Red Sea*

What Is It? *The Story of Manna in the Desert*

A Tall Wall *The Story of Jericho*

A Baby for Hannah *The Story of an Answered Prayer*

Samuel! Samuel! *The Story of God's Call to Samuel*

Lions and Bears! *The Story of David the Shepherd Boy*

David and the Giant *The Story of David and Goliath*

A Little Jar of Oil *The Story of Elisha and the Widow*

One, Two, Three, Four, Five, Six, Seven! *The Story of Elisha and Naaman*

A Big Fish Story *The Story of Jonah*

Lions, Lions! *The Story of Daniel*

New Testament Stories

Jesus Is Born! *The Story of Christmas*

Good News! *The Story of the Shepherds*

An Amazing Star! *The Story of the Wise Men*

Waiting, Waiting, Waiting! *The Story of Simeon and Anna*

Who Is This Child? *The Story of Jesus in the Temple*

Follow Me! *The Story of Jesus and His Twelve Helpers*

The Greatest Gift *The Story of Jesus and the Woman at the Well*

A Father's Wish *The Story of Jesus and a Little Boy*

Just Believe! *The Story of Jesus and a Little Girl*

Get Up and Walk! *The Story of Jesus and a Man Who Couldn't Walk*

A Little Lunch *The Story of Jesus and a Hungry Crowd*

A Scary Storm *The Story of Jesus and a Stormy Sea*

Thank You, Jesus! *The Story of Jesus and One Thankful Man*

A Wonderful Sight! *The Story of Jesus and a Man Who Couldn't See*

A Better Thing to Do *The Story of Jesus and Mary and Martha*

A Lost Lamb *The Story of the Good Shepherd*

Come to Me! *The Story of Jesus and the Children*

Have a Great Day! *The Story of Jesus and Zacchaeus*

I Love You, Jesus! *The Story of Mary's Gift to Jesus*

Hosanna! *The Story of Palm Sunday*

The Best Day Ever! *The Story of Easter*

Goodbye—for Now *The Story of Jesus' Return to Heaven*

A Prayer for Peter *The Story of Peter in Prison*

Sad Day, Happy Day! *The Story of Peter and Dorcas*

A New Friend *The Story of Paul's Conversion*

Over the Wall *The Story of Paul's Escape in a Basket*

A Song in the Night *The Story of Paul and Silas in Prison*

A Ride in the Night *The Story of Paul's Escape on Horseback*

The Shipwreck *The Story of Paul's Rescue at Sea*

Holiday Stories

Selected stories from the New Testament to help you celebrate the Christian year

Jesus Is Born! *The Story of Christmas*

Good News! *The Story of the Shepherds*

An Amazing Star! *The Story of the Wise Men*

Hosanna! *The Story of Palm Sunday*

The Best Day Ever! *The Story of Easter*

Goodbye—for Now *The Story of Jesus' Return to Heaven*

These fifty-two books are the heart of *God Loves Me*, a Bible story program designed for young children. Individual books (or the entire set) and the accompanying program guide *God Loves Me* are available from CRC Publications (1-800-333-8300).